D0821317

Seals on Wheels

Seals on Wheels By Dean Walley

Illustrated by Michele Shulte

♔ Hallmark Children's Editions

A First Book About Colors

Red seals.

Orange wheels.

Seals on wheels.

Goodbye seals. Goodbye wheels.

Green meanies roasting wienies.

Meanies jump in yellow jello.

They turn into yellow fellows.

Small blue snail.

Big blue whale.

Snail on whale.   Whale on snail?

It's no wonder they go under.

Plates of purple pickle pie.
Pink peacock passing by.

When he's full of pickle pie,
Pink peacock says,
"Goodbye."

A pair of bright white alligators.
This white gator is a waiter.

This white gator is a skater.

Skater gator, waiter gator say,
"Goodbye,

We'll see you later."

Night is falling. Bang!

It's black now.

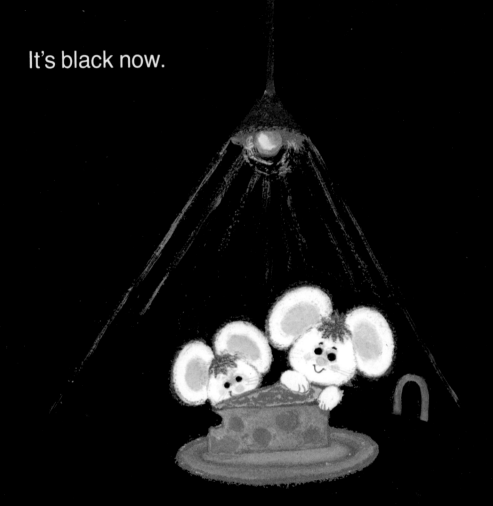

Shall we have a bedtime snack now?